You who live safe
In your warm houses,
You who find, returning in the evening,
Hot food and friendly faces:
 Consider if this is a man
 Who works in the mud
 Who does not know peace
 Who fights for a scrap of bread
 Who dies because of a yes or a no.
 Consider if this is a woman,
 Without hair and without name
 With no more strength to remember,
 Her eyes empty and her womb cold
 Like a frog in winter.
Meditate that this came about:
I commend these words to you.
Carve them in your hearts
At home, in the street,
Going to bed, rising;
Repeat them to your children,
 Or may your house fall apart,
 May illness impede you,
 May your children turn their faces from you.

    Primo Levi 1919-1987
    Survival in Auschwitz
    Committed suicde
    on April 11, 1987

    April 11, 1926
    This book's author was born

The Liberation of the
Concentration Camps 1945

The Des Moines, Iowa
Survivors

Never Forget!

Adele Anolik

Adele A. Anolik

Ice Cube Press
North Liberty, Iowa

This book previously appeared in different form in 1995 as a
50th Anniversary Commemoration on The Liberation of The
Concentration Camps as a project of the Jewish Community
Relations Commission of the Jewish Federation of Greater Des
Moines.

Thanks to the following people for their help: Cover drawing by
Deborah Pappenheimer. Cover photo of Jewish Monument and the
Dobrin gravestone were taken by David Anolik. 1939 map of Europe
created by Martin Cassell. Permission to use photo of Michael
Dobrin's gravestone provided graciously by his family: Michele,
Eva & Sonia Dobrin. A special thanks to my daughter, Julie Anolik
Cassell, who, through her friendship with this publisher and his
family, has made this 2nd edition possible, making it available to
readers outside the Des Moines Community.

"Please know that I was moved to read of the many years you devoted to documenting the tragedies of the Holocaust. Thank you for helping preserve memory with such a deep level of commitment"
—Elie Wiesel, letter to Mrs. Anolik

"This book is a moving testimonial to Jews who survived the Holocaust and came to live long and prosper in Iowa. These are important tales of how the uprooted of Europe sank new roots in the rich soil of America's heartland."
—Dr. Harry Brod, Professor of Philosophy and Humanities, University of Northern Iowa, Editor, *The Legacy of the Holocaust: Children and the Holocaust*

"I showed the book to the group of survivors that meet at the Center periodically ... 'It's like a holy siddur' was their first response."
—Dr. Arthur Flug, Executive Director of the Holocaust Resource Center and Archives at the City University of New York's Queensborough Community College

TABLE OF CONTENTS

FOREWORD

It is appropriate that Mom chose Primo Levi's words to introduce her book. For me these words read as a guiding principle behind how Holocaust survivors raised their kids.

I believe my sister Lisa, brother David and I were raised to "never forget" and to "remember" as the title of this book denotes. It is without question that we too have raised our children to never forget and to remember.

I think anyone who reads this book will never forget either.

Julie Anolik Cassell
(author's daughter)
July, 2008

INTRODUCTION

In 1981, Helen Mischkiet-Edell and her husband Mark Edell diverted a portion of the estate bequeathed to Helen by her recently deceased parents towards the establishment of the Mischkiet-Spiler Holocaust Education Fund. Administered by the Jewish Community Relations Commission (JCRC) of Greater Des Moines, the Mischkiet-Spiler Fund has enabled the local Jewish community to initiate a number of Holocaust-related educational projects, including this 50th anniversary commemoration. Through their generous gift to the JCRC, Helen and Mark hoped to accomplish several things. They first and foremost wished to ensure that the term "never again" remains a reality and that the lessons of the Holocaust do not fade with time. They also desired to honor the memory of Helen's parents, Fela and Monek Mischkiet, and their dear friend and fellow Holocaust-survivor Selman Spiler. This, then, is the Mischkiet-Spiler story:

Fela Plachinsky was born in Lodz, Poland in the year 1910. She came from a middle-class family of eight brothers and sisters. Monek Mischkiet came from a small Polish town called Yanov. He was born in 1906, and also came from a middle-class family of eight brothers and sisters. Monek did not take on his father's trade as a baker, but instead chose to become a tailor. As Lodz was a large textile city, he moved there to practice his profession. In 1935, Fela and Monek were married as a result of the efforts of a "Shadchan," or Jewish matchmaker. Monek opened up his own tailor shop and Fela continued to work as a dressmaker until the birth of their daughter Bayla.

After the Nazi invasion of 1939, the Jews of Poland were forced into re-created medieval ghettos where deliberate malnutrition and overcrowding were the order of the day. In 1942, Fela's and Monek's daughter Bayla died of typhus. Two years later, the Lodz Ghetto was liquidated, and Fela and Monek were deported to the infamous death camp at Auschwitz. At Auschwitz, the Mischkiets escaped the gas chambers because the Nazis considered them robust enough to work. Monek was sent to Dachau while Fela was sent to a series of camps closer to the Russian border, including the camp of Stutthof. Both Fela and Monek managed to survive the war as slave laborers in concentration camps where they manufactured uniforms for the German army.

In May 1945, Fela and Monek were liberated by the advancing Allies. Following Fela's liberation, she went to work for the European branch of the Haganah, the Jewish underground defense force in Palestine. Fela's mission was to identify and retrieve Jewish children who had been hidden in Catholic convents during the war. The Haganah would then attempt to smuggle these orphaned Jewish children through the British Navy blockade into Palestine. One day, a Haganah co-worker discovered Monek's name listed in the Bad Tolz City Hall's "Book of the Living". Monek and his friend Selman Spiler had been liberated in May of 1945 and had been living in that city. Upon hearing this news, Fela went to Bad Tolz where the Mischkiets were reunited. In Bad Tolz, the Mischkiets and Selman Spiler regained their health and continued to live and work for the next several years.

In 1951, Fela and Monek were granted visas to the United States when sponsorships became available through the Des Moines Jewish Federation. Upon their arrival in Des Moines, they were greeted at the train station by Mr. and Mrs. Fred

Badower. Fred Badower was also a tailor in Lodz and knew Fela and Monek while living in the ghetto. A few months later, a second daughter, Helen, was born to them. Monek immediately went to work as the tailor in a local cleaning establishment and continued to be a tailor until his death in 1980.

Fela and Monek were unusually willing to talk about their wartime experiences with customers, friends and their daughter's classmates. In 1969, PBS asked the Mischkiets' permission to produce a documentary about their life during the Holocaust. The network learned of the Mischkiets through a story in the *Des Moines Register* about their daughter playing the role of Anne in *The Diary of Anne Frank* at North High School.

Selman (Sol) Spiler was born in 1907 in Kovno, Lithuania. During his youth, Selman was very involved in Yiddish theater and sports. He led a normal life as a dental technician, was married and had a son. When the war broke out, it did not take the Nazis long to ghettoize Kovno. Like many other Jewish husbands, Selman was permanently separated from his wife and son when he was deported to Dachau in 1943. While in Dachau, he soon befriended Monek Mischkiet. They both worked making uniforms for Nazi soldiers: Spiler as the cutter and Mischkiet as the tailor. They developed a friendship that would last throughout the remainder of their lives.

After the camp was liberated by American soldiers in 1945, the two men stayed together in the town of Bad Tolz, Germany. They were nursed back to health and began their new lives. It was during this time that Selman learned of the possibility that his wife and son had survived the war and were living in Russia. He was never able, however, to substantiate this claim. In 1952, Spiler came to Des Moines to join the Mischkiets. He immediately began working as a dental technician and eventually opened his own practice. His passion for Yiddish theater and music manifested itself in his election as president of the Des Moines Jewish Culture Club. During his presidency Spiler was determined to have a monument erected in memory of the six million Jewish men, women and children who perished in the Holocaust. (This monument is located in the Glendale Cemetery, 4909 University Ave., Des Moines, Iowa; see photo shown on back cover.) Selman wanted everyone to remember the Holocaust and the lessons this tragedy held for mankind: the world must never forget or repeat such a horror. He actively campaigned for the realization of this project, mobilizing resources of the Des Moines community of survivors. The monument was dedicated in ceremonies held in 1960. Although not a religious man, Spiler maintained an active interest in the State of Israel and World Jewry. Selman died on June 1, 1979, in Des Moines, Iowa.

Fela and Monek Mischkiet

Selman Spiler and Monek Mischkiet

State of Iowa
Executive Department

PROCLAMATION

WHEREAS, between the years 1933 and 1945, six million Jewish men, women and children were systematically killed by the Nazi German regime and its collaborators in a program of industrialized mass murder for no other reason than the fact that these innocent victims had been born Jews; and

WHEREAS, the Romani Gypsies, Slavs, the handicapped, political and religious dissidents also suffered and died at the hands of Hitler and his minions; and

WHEREAS, May 11, 1995, marks the fifty second anniversary of the uprising by valiant young Jewish men and women in the Warsaw Ghetto against overwhelming German military might; and that the Warsaw Ghetto Uprising was the first in a series of armed rebellions conducted by Jews against their Nazi tormentors at the death camps of Treblinka and Sobibor; and that Jewish partisans waged a courageous campaign of guerrilla warfare against German forces throughout Nazi-occupied Europe; and

WHEREAS, the date of the Warsaw Ghetto Uprising has been declared "Yom Hashoah," an international day of Holocaust remembrance; and the citizens of Iowa should remember the crimes against humanity perpetrated by Nazi Germany as the most severe manifestation of bigotry and intolerance in recorded human history; and all Iowans should recognize that hatred provides a breeding ground for tyranny to flourish:

NOW, THEREFORE, I, Terry E. Branstad, Governor of the State of Iowa, in memory of the victims of the Shoah and in the hope that we will always strive to overcome all forms of prejudice and inhumanity through education, vigilance and resistance to oppression, do hereby proclaim the week of Sunday, May 7 through Sunday, May 14, 1995, as

DAYS OF REMEMBRANCE FOR THE VICTIMS OF THE SHOAH

in the State of Iowa.

IN TESTIMONY WHEREOF, I have hereunto subscribed my name and caused the Great Seal of the State of Iowa to be affixed. Done at Des Moines, this 11th day of the Hebrew month of Iyar, in the Hebrew year five thousand seven hundred fifty five; this 11th day of May in the year one thousand nine hundred and ninety five.

Terry E. Branstad
GOVERNOR

ATTEST:

Paul D. Pate
Secretary of State

REPLY TO:

☐ 135 HART SENATE OFFICE BUILDING
WASHINGTON, DC 20510-1501
(202) 224-3744
TTY: (202) 224-4479

☐ 721 FEDERAL BUILDING
210 WALNUT STREET
DES MOINES, IA 50309-2140
(515) 284-4890

☐ 206 FEDERAL BUILDING
101 1ST STREET SE.
CEDAR RAPIDS, IA 52401-1227
(319) 363-6832

REPLY TO:

☐ 103 FEDERAL COURTHOUSE Bu
320 6TH STREET
SIOUX CITY, IA 51101-1244
(712) 233-1860

☐ 210 WATERLOO BUILDING
531 COMMERCIAL STREET
WATERLOO, IA 50701-5497
(319) 232-6657

☐ 116 FEDERAL BUILDING
131 E. 4TH STREET
DAVENPORT, IA 52801-1513
(319) 322-4331

☐ 307 FEDERAL BUILDING
8 SOUTH 6TH STREET
COUNCIL BLUFFS, IA 51501
(712) 322-7103

United States Senate

CHARLES E. GRASSLEY

WASHINGTON, DC 20510-1501

April 5, 1995

Jewish Community Relations Commission
910 Polk Boulevard
Des Moines, Iowa 50312-2297

Dear Friends:

I would like to send my regards to you on the commemoration of
the coming Yom Hashoah which will take place on the 50th
anniversary of the end of the Second World War and the liberation
of the Nazi death camps. I would like to take this opportunity
to salute the long-standing and strong tradition of the Jewish
Federation. I applaud the Jewish Community Relations Committee
for your devotion, and for organizing the activities scheduled
for Thursday, May 11, 1995, commemorating this important
anniversary.

Organizations such as yours play an instrumental role as we
strive to promote greater awareness and respect for Survivors and
Liberators of World War II concentration camps. It is also
important for generations to come to learn of such
extraordinarily horrifying war-time experiences so they will not
have to live through them again in the future. The leadership
you have demonstrated is greatly appreciated. The Federation has
made a positive difference in our state of Iowa and we are
grateful for the spirit of community service which the Jewish
Federation embodies.

Thank you and I wish your organization great success in future
endeavors.

Sincerely,

Chuck

Charles E. Grassley
United States Senator

Keep up the good work!

Committee Assignments:

Senator Tom Harkin

May 11, 1995

50th Anniversary of Yom Hoshoah

Dear Friends:

It is a privilege for me to join all of you in commemorating the 50th Anniversary of Yom Hashoah. This is truly a special day and I am proud to mark this important event.

Today is, above all, a day of remembrance. Half a century ago, American and other allied soldiers put an end to the unspeakable horror of the concentration camps. Through the eyes of the liberators--and those who survived the torture of the camps--the world witnessed tragedy beyond the realm of human comprehension.

Although those images first became a part of the world consciousness fifty years ago, they remain just as painful and real today. That is, in large part, due to your continuing work to ensure that the world always remembers that awful period so that we may never relive it.

Let us continue to stand together in the constant effort to be eternally vigilant against the destructive forces of racism, prejudice and intolerance.

My thanks to the Des Moines Jewish Community Relations Commission for hosting this event, and my best wishes to you all.

Sincerely,

Tom

Tom Harkin
United States Senator

GREG GANSKE
4TH DISTRICT, IOWA

COMMERCE COMMITTEE
SUBCOMMITTEES:
HEALTH AND ENVIRONMENT
COMMERCE, TRADE, AND HAZARDOUS
MATERIALS

CONGRESS OF THE UNITED STATES
HOUSE OF REPRESENTATIVES

March 29, 1995

The Jewish Federation of
  Greater Des Moines
910 Polk Boulevard
Des Moines, Iowa 50312

Dear Friends:

    I am very proud to join in commemorating the end of World War II. It was a conflict which inflicted unthinkable devastation across the globe. Aside from the enormous number of fatalities among armed services, millions of innocent men, women, and children lost their lives.

    Claiming the lives of approximately twelve million people, the Holocaust was an appallingly destructive effort to remove various races and religions from the world. Half of the victims of this campaign of violence were Jews.

    We are all familiar with the old saying that "those who forget the past are doomed to repeat it." It is unfortunate that in the half-century since the end of World War II, we have failed to eliminate bigotry and ethnic cleansing. As we struggle with many of these issues around the world, I salute your efforts to keep alive the memory of the Holocaust, both its victims and its survivors.

    Once again, my best wishes to my friends in the Jewish Community on the fiftieth anniversary of the end of the Second World War. Let us hope that in the next fifty years, we better learn to live in peace with our neighbors.

Sincerely,

Greg Ganske, M.D.
Member of Congress

1108 LONGWORTH HOUSE OFFICE BUILDING
WASHINGTON, DC 20515
(202) 225-4426

FEDERAL BUILDING
210 WALNUT STREET
DES MOINES, IA 50309
(515) 284-4634

40 PEARL STREET
COUNCIL BLUFFS, IA 515
(712) 323-5976

PRINTED ON RECYCLED PAPER

The Des Moines, Iowa Survivors

The inscription on this gravestone reflects a
sentiment shared by those in this book:

*"This monument stands as a memorial to Michael
Dobrin who miraculously survived that whirlwind
of destruction called the holocaust which claimed
the lives of his parents Zelda and Chaim and sister
Sonja may their memories be always a blessing."*

Map of 1939 Europe indicating both where the survivors were born and the primary concentration camps mentioned in this book.

CHARLES (CHAIM) ANOLIK

Charles was born to Yakov and Mina Anolik, the oldest of three sons. His father worked as an engineer constructing church cupolas, and his mother was a homemaker. Charles attended a Hebrew Gymnasium.

In 1940 the Russians occupied Lithuania in what was essentially a peaceful take-over. On June 22, 1941, the Germans came and bombarded the airport. That same night the local Lithuanian population began ransacking Jewish homes, killing over one thousand Jews. At about this same time, Charles' younger brother, Baruch, attempted to escape but was caught and killed by Lithuanians who were collaborating with the Nazi campaign of genocide against the Jews. The following day the German Army marched in. Two days later, going house to house, the Germans took twenty-three young Jewish girls, raped them, then killed them and returned them to the Jewish community for burial. One of the girls killed was Charles' girlfriend.

On July 6, 1941, the Lithuanian National basketball team won a victory against the German army team. To celebrate, the German commandant gave permission for each Lithuanian player to kill ten Jews.

In 1941, Charles and his parents were forced into the Slobotka Ghetto near Kaunas. All the able-bodied people had to go out daily to work on the air-base or wherever they were needed. In October, Charles' father was taken from the ghetto and shot. In 1942, all the children who were imprisoned in the ghetto were murdered, including Charles' four year-old nephew. In 1941, 40,000 Jews were ghettoized. When the ghetto was liquidated in 1943, less than 800 Jews remained. In 1943, Charles, his mother, brother and sister-in-law were sent to Palemonas, a concentration camp in

Lithuania where they worked in a brick factory. In 1944 his family was shipped to Dachau in cattle cars. At Dachau the men and women were separated, the women going to Stutthof and the men remaining in Dachau. Prisoners worked on the Reichsautobahn and an underground airplane hangar for the Messerschmidt Airplane Factory.

In 1945, Charles and his brother, Ben, were forced to go on a death march to the Bavarian Alps to build fortifications for the retreating German Army. Hundreds died on the four-day march. At one point Ben couldn't walk any further, so Charles stayed behind with him and about 15 others. They dug their graves that night, expecting to be shot. Because of the late hour the Germans decided to wait until morning before organizing a firing squad. That night the location was overrun by advancing US troops. When the Americans arrived, the Germans had fled. The Americans, not knowing what to do with the living skeletons, gave them food. Many died of diarrhea. Charles and his brother survived.

After a year's hospitalization, Charles worked in Munich from 1945 to 1949 as a bookkeeper for JOINT (Jewish Joint Distribution Committee) and studied at the university at night. In May 1949, with exit papers sent by a cousin, Charles came to America. After deciding to become a cosmetologist, he worked in Fifth Avenue salons until opening his own salon in Des Moines, Iowa. On New Year's Eve, 1955, while visiting friends in Chicago, Charles met Adele Waldner from Kansas City. They married the following September. Charles and Adele have two daughters, one son and four grandchildren.

Born in Kaunas, Lithuania

FRED (EFRAIM FISCHL) BADOWER

Fred was born to Wolf and Chaya Badower in Lodz, a large city in central Poland. He was the second oldest of nine children, five girls and four boys. During army service, his father was trained to be a tailor and made military clothing under the supervision of his Russian general boss. Beginning at age nine Fred was taught tailoring by his father and by age 13 could make an entire garment.

In 1936 Fred married for the first time and after one year the Badowers had a baby boy. In 1939 the Germans came and all the Jews were herded into a ghetto where living conditions were indescribable. The ghetto was created by fencing in a slum, clearing out the Poles and putting them in formerly Jewish homes. Food in the ghetto was limited to soup. Tailor shops were set up to sew uniforms for German soldiers. Fred's wife had to work. If you didn't work you didn't get the day's ration of soup. In order to feed the baby, Fred would eat his ration of soup one day; the next day he fed his ration of soup to the baby. His wife did the same. Fred's father died of starvation trying to save food for his children.

Then came the order to take out of the ghetto those who could not work. Included in this order were the children and the elderly. No one believed the children would be murdered. But the old and the young were gassed, including Fred's four-and-a-half year old son. His wife did not survive.

Because of the need for slave labor, Fred and his mother were among those transported to Auschwitz where they were separated upon arrival. His mother was sent to the gas chamber on the right and Fred went to the left. He described his stay in Auschwitz as brief, but terrible. Three days later he was deported to Kaufering, then Dachau and Kempten, where kapos (prisoner-helpers) assisted the Germans in beating and murdering those who disobeyed camp regulations. Fred's group was sent to work in the woods. Beatings would occur for such minor infractions as sinking into the mud.

In 1945 the Americans liberated Dachau and Fred went to work as a tailor in Munich. It was here that he learned that one brother and two sisters had survived. While in Munich, in 1949, Fred worked for a US agency and was helped by a friend there to obtain a passport. So without further delay, and deciding not to wait for a passport to Australia where he had friends, Fred left for America. Met by an agency representative, he was sent to Des Moines where he was greeted by Charles Anolik at the train station.

After his arrival in Des Moines, Fred worked in a local tailor's shop. There he met and later married Anne Cohen. At this point, Fred opened a clothing shop in his home and, after the birth of his daughter Helen in 1952, the Badowers moved the store to the Roosevelt Shopping Center. In 1956 their son Michael was born. The Ingersoll store came later and still bears the Badower name.

Born on January 4, 1909, in Lodz, Poland (deceased)

DAVID FISHEL

David was born to parents Ben and Ryfka Fishel, and was the youngest of five children. He had two brothers and two sisters. David's father manufactured shirts and his mother was a homemaker. His father died when David was five years old. The family remained in Breslau, Germany until 1935 when, due to anti-Semitic violence against the large Jewish population, they moved to Bedzin in Poland. Here David attended Folk School until 1939 when German troops entered the town. He had to leave school at age 11 because he was Jewish. At this time, David's family was forced to relocate into a single room. In September 1939, David was taken into forced labor in Bedzin where he remained until 1942. Both brothers were deported. In 1941 his mother, both sisters, a brother-in-law and a niece were deported and never seen again.

From March until December 1942, David was transferred to Bismarckhiitte. It should be noted that transfers were always done in boxcars or on foot. From December 1942 until December 1943 he was sent to Regensfeld. From December 1943 until January 1945 he was in Blechhammer. All the foregoing were forced slave labor camps, primarily to serve the I.G. Farben factory (an infamous factory which made synthetic oils, rubber and Zyklon B—the lethal gas used in the concentration camps).

From Blechhammer came a forced march to Gross-Rosen where he witnessed an SS officer killing prisoners with his bare hands. Then there were transports to Buchenwald and Langenstein bei Halberstadt where he hid among dead bodies to avoid the camp's evacuation. At this time, David was only 17 years old. He was tattooed with two numbers— one from Auschwitz and one from Buchenwald—although he was never actually in Auschwitz. David was liberated by American troops on April 11, 1945. After a recuperation period at Halberstadt, he was transferred to the Displaced Persons Camp at Bergen-Belsen. At Belsen he found one of his brothers, the only member of his immediate family who survived.

By a strange coincidence, in 1947 his picture came to the attention of an aunt living in Omaha, Nebraska. She sent papers for David and his brother to come to the United States, and he did so six weeks later. His brother came one month later, after getting married in Germany. In 1951 David met Louise Fagen from Des Moines who was visiting friends. They were married in Des Moines in 1952 and in the ensuing years had two daughters who now live out of state. They have four grandchildren.

In 1963 David opened Fishel's Delicatessen. He still works and is owner of a landmark Deli on the Skywalk in downtown Des Moines. In recent years David has somewhat overcome his reluctance to talk to people about the de-humanization of Jews. He is one of the few people in our Survivor community who has undertaken the job of educating students.

Born on September 22, 1928, in Breslau, Germany, now Poland (deceased)

LINDA RINGERMACHER FISHMAN

Linda was born to parents Ghana and Yitzak Ringermacher, who ran a butcher shop out of their home in a Polish *shtetl* (small Jewish village). She was the fifth of seven children, having four older sisters and two younger brothers.

In 1941 the parents' business was confiscated and they were taken forcibly to Radom, Poland, and jailed there, leaving seven young children to struggle for themselves until sometime in 1942. Then one day the Germans ordered that one family member from each house go out to work for two hours, and Linda took it upon herself to go. She never saw her family again. She was taken away to an ammunitions factory in Skarzisko, 10 kilometers from home. Two weeks later she became ill with typhus, was taken to a hospital, and nearly died.

While in the hospital area for prisoners, an Uncle Aaron who lived nearby paid a doctor to treat Linda and insisted she come home with him to recover. Linda refused and instead returned to the camp, although still very ill. She walked two kilometers back to the camp and in doing so made the most important decision of her life. Two days later all the hospitalized prisoners were murdered. And her fears for the safety of her family were based in reality: all were transported to Treblinka, where they were gassed.

After two and one-half years in Skarzisko, Linda was taken successively to Buchenwald (briefly), Bergen-Belsen (five months), and two smaller camps. It was from the last of the camps that the prisoners were forced to go on a death march to Dachau. They were turned away because of lack of space. They were then forced to march ten kilometers to Allach, located midway between Dachau and Munich and were liberated by the American Seventh Army in May,

1945. While Linda was still in Allach, Ansel Fishman, who had been liberated from Dachau, came looking for cousins, but instead found Linda Ringermacher. They were married in Allach on December 24, 1945, and it was here that their daughter Ann was born. When Ann was nine months old they emigrated to the United States with the help of HIAS (Hebrew Immigrant Aid Society) on July 14, 1950, and were re-settled in Des Moines. Sons Morris and Steven were born here.

Linda and Ansel opened an upholstery business in 1953. Ansel died in 1970, never having come to terms with the atrocities experienced in the camps. We are fortunate to have Linda as one of our principal spokespersons to educate students and adults alike that we must never forget.

Born in Szydlowiec, Poland

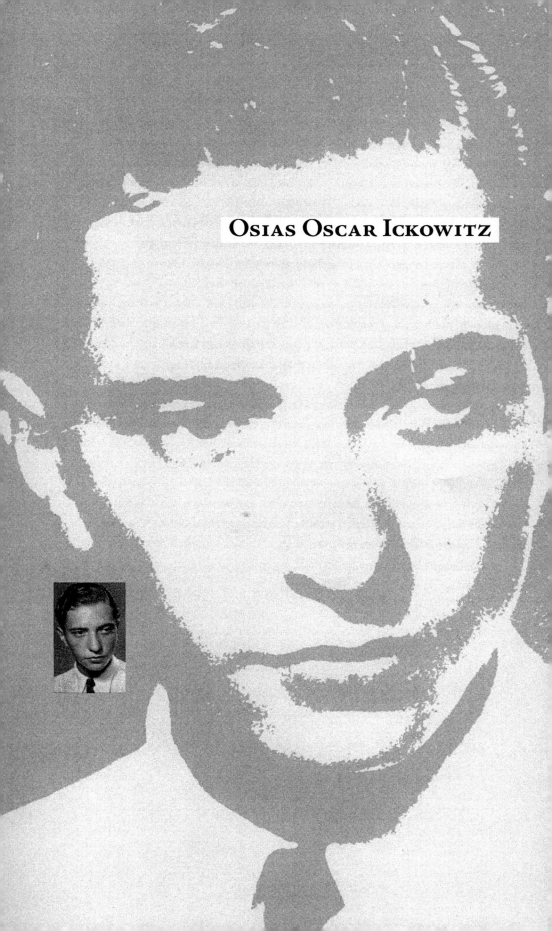

OSIAS OSCAR ICKOWITZ

Oscar was born to parents Rebecca and David Ickowitz, the fifth youngest of nine children, five brothers and three sisters. His mother was a homemaker, having the responsibility for nine children. His father was an artisan, a highly skilled furrier, who was often called to provide furs for the Queen of Rumania.

In 1940 the Germans came to Bucharest. In 1941 they started transporting the Jews out of Romania to concentration camps in the Ukraine and the Crimea, and Oscar was sent to a camp in Mogilev. The prisoners were responsible for cleaning streets and keeping cities cleared of the destruction wrought by the war. The rest of the family was split up and sent to other camps in the same area of Russia. It was in Mogilev that Oscar spent the years from September 1941 to Passover in April 1944, at which time Jews were repatriated to Bucharest after being liberated by the Russians.

An intense search for his parents was successful, but he found them ill and they did not survive for long. The search for siblings was more successful. In Bucharest he found all of his brothers and sisters, and the entire family remained there until 1946. It was also in 1946 that Oscar married his childhood girlfriend Jane, and together they went to Admont, Austria, the first of several Displaced Persons camps, where their first son Angelo was born. The next Displaced Persons camps were in Salzburg, Austria; Airing, Germany; and Traunstein, Bavaria. It was in Traunstein that sons Morris and David were born. The continual change of camps was necessitated by severely overcrowded conditions. Finally they were taken to Felderfink, Germany, where they remained until they came to the United States in 1951, with the help of JOINT (Jewish Joint Distribution Committee).

Jane and Oscar were re-settled in Des Moines, Iowa. They were met at the train by Mr. Spiegelman of the Jewish Federation. Daughter Rose was born in 1953. Oscar's first job was with Younkers, which he left for a time, but to which he returned and where he worked for 25 years until he retired. His wife Jane died in 1989. His son David was killed in an automobile accident in 1994, leaving behind six children.

August 27, 1924, in Bucharest, Romania (deceased)

Irvin Karp

Irvin was born to parents Leon and Cyrtia Karp. His mother died at an early age. There were seven children in his family: four boys and three girls. Irvin was next to the youngest. His older brother David moved to the United States in 1911. Another brother moved to Palestine in 1931, and the youngest brother eventually moved to what is now Israel after the war. Irvin's father, an engineer, remarried and moved to Palestine in 1932, where he remained until his death in 1942. None of Irvin's sisters survived.

In his youth, Irvin attended a Polish school from which he graduated and became a bookkeeper. He worked in a company where his future wife's father was a customer. Then in 1924 Irvin met Phyllis Wittenberg. They both worked in Radomsko as bookkeepers until 1929 when they married and moved to Krakow, where Irvin found work as the accountant/manager in Hogo, a large Jewish-owned haberdashery company.

In 1931, when daughter Celina was born, there were already indications of anti-Semitic activity. However, the Karps remained in Krakow until September 1939 when the Germans entered Poland and proceeded to take over Hogo, which now became a factory for the production of Army materiel. The Karps were able to stay in their Krakow apartment until 1941, when the Germans rounded up Jews and forcibly marched them into the ghetto. Those who managed to survive lived in crowded, filthy conditions and many died of starvation.

On March 13, 1943, the Krakow Ghetto was liquidated and prisoners were marched to Krakow-Plaszow, a work camp with four barracks. Phyllis remembers this as a cemetery. The men and women were separated. Irvin remained there until October 1944 at which time he was transported to Gross-

Rosen, Germany. Irvin remained there until, through the artifice of Oskar Schindler (a German industrialist credited with saving as many as 1,300 Jews during the Holocaust, by having them work in his factories located in what is now Poland and the Czech Republic), he was moved out to Briinnlitz, Czechoslovakia—one of 120 men on Schlindler's list. In Briinnlitz the family was reunited and on May 9, 1945, they were liberated by the Russians.

A detailed account of their emigration to the United States can be read in the reminiscences of Phyllis Karp (*pp.* 44-45). Irvin worked in Des Moines for the H.E. Sorensen Company for 17 years, where he was office and credit manager. He retired in 1975.

Born on January 2, 1903, in Radomkso, Poland (deceased)

PHYLLIS (FEIGE WITTENBERG) KARP

Phyllis was born to parents Shmule and Zysia Wittenberg. There were six children in the family: three girls and three boys. Phyllis was the middle sister. Her parents owned a wholesale/retail grocery store. Phyllis graduated from a Jewish Gymnasium, then worked in a Jewish bank as a bookkeeper.

In 1929 she met Irvin Karp. They married on September 15, 1929, and moved to Krakow. At that time Phyllis worked as a bookkeeper in a big Krakow winery. Daughter Celina was born in 1931. She was in third grade in September 1939 when the Germans invaded Poland. In Radomsko, Phyllis' parents and one brother, along with her older sister and four children, were killed by a bomb on the first day of the occupation. Her oldest brother had moved to Palestine in 1918 and one brother was killed in France during the war.

The Karps remained in the city of Krakow until 1941, when the Germans forcibly moved all Jews to the ghetto. Phyllis recalls an incident in the ghetto when German Captain Amon Goeth gave orders for parents to leave the ghetto for barracks nearby. Children were to be left, but would be returned to parents the following day. Although Goeth had given his word, Phyllis was not convinced and managed to get Celina out with the large group of adults by making her up to look older. Goeth did keep his word. The following day 800 dead children were returned to their parents for burial.

When the Krakow Ghetto was liquidated in March 1943, Phyllis and Celina were shipped in cattle cars to Auschwitz, where the men and women were separated. Here they managed to survive, under sub-human conditions, including abuse and starvation, until 1944, when they were transported to Briinnlitz, Czechoslovakia, part of the group of 300 women who were rescued from Auschwitz by the calculated dealings of Oskar Schindler. At Briinnlitz, Mrs. Schindler was responsible for helping the ill by bringing food in each morning. Phyllis gives Mrs. Schindler credit for saving Celina's life. Irvin had also been transported to Briinnlitz, thanks to Schindler, and here the family remained until liberated by the Russians on May 9, 1945.

After the liberation, the Karps returned briefly to Poland in the hope of finding Phyllis' younger sister, but learned that she had been murdered in Stutthof concentration camp. On July 4, 1946, 46 Jews were murdered by the local non-Jewish Polish population in the infamous Kielce pogrom. Having no desire to remain in Poland following this atrocity, they smuggled themselves out first to Czechoslovakia, then to Germany. In Mendelheim they were able to obtain passports through JOINT (Jewish Joint Distribution Committee) and also made contact with Irvin's brother David, who had come to the United States in 1911.

In 1947, the Karps came to America and re-settled in Des Moines, where Phyllis worked as an accountant for Peat Marwick until her retirement in 1975. She also worked for Louis Nussbaum. Her daughter Celina lives in California.

Born in Radomsko, Poland (deceased)

Helga (Lindemann, Levy) Krongelb

Helga was born to parents Henrietta and Joseph Lindemann. Joseph was a successful merchant in the furniture business. Her mother, Henrietta, died in 1930. Helga had one older brother who was killed in a concentration camp, whereabouts unknown. She attended a Jewish school for four years and later a German Gymnasium. During most of her youth, Helga lived in Gelsenkirchen, but did travel and work in Essen and other cities as a buyer for clothing stores.

On August 17, 1939, Helga married Paul Levy in her hometown. They remained there until 1942 when the Nazis rounded up the local German Jews and deported them. She was taken to Stutthof, Poland, but she doesn't know where Paul was taken. He did not survive. Her father, who had remarried, was taken to a concentration camp—Kaiserwald, she thinks—where he died.

Helga remained in Stutthof until close to the liberation. Then one night she and a friend escaped and made their way to Bromberg, Poland, where they remained until the war ended in 1945. From Bromberg the two went to Berlin, always looking for familiar faces. Finding no one, they returned to Gelsenkirchen and then to Bremen, where Helga set up a Jewish Old Age Home. The Jewish Committee in Bremen, provided them with financial assistance to buy the necessities they required to sustain them. JOINT (Jewish Joint Distribution Committee) made arrangements for their emigration to the United States in 1951. Her friend remained in New York until the time of her death, not too long afterward.

Helga was re-settled in Des Moines and makes note of the fact that she arrived very much alone and without anyone to meet her at the station. However, Mr. Spiegelman from the

Federation soon had her working at the Iowa Jewish Home for the Aged, as it was then called, and she became a very important part of the community.

In 1957 Helga married Simon Krongelb, who had been in a concentration camp in Warsaw, as a Pole. After the war he went to Bremen where he had great difficulty proving he was Jewish, proof which he needed in order to get assistance from JOINT so he could come to the United States. He arrived in Des Moines two months before Helga. Simon died in 1983.

Helga worked at the Iowa Jewish Home for the Aged until retirement in 1975.

Born on October 11, 1912, in Gelsenkirchen, Germany

PAULA (RUPPEL BORUCHOVITZ) MURAWNIK

Paula was born in Gorzda to parents Yosef and Bela Ruppel. She was the fourth youngest of eleven children. She had three brothers and seven sisters. Her father was a shoemaker and her mother a homemaker. After attending Folk School, Paula moved to Memel, a predominantly German city occupied by Lithuania in 1922. It was an industrialized port city and provided the rare opportunity for young workers from small cities to obtain employment. It was here that Paula worked in a cigarette factory until Hitler came to Memel in 1938.

In 1939 Paula returned to Gorzda to see her mother; her father had already died. Not too long after her arrival, Paula's mother died in an accidental drowning. After a brief period Paula left for Kovno (Kaunas) and once again worked in a cigarette factory. While there she met Abe Boruchovitz, who later became her husband. In 1941 the German Army entered the city and on June 22 bombarded the airport. Many people, including Paula, ran away to other cities. She stopped in a city already occupied by the Germans who, zealously assisted by the local Lithuanians, were ransacking Jewish homes and killing Jews. She stayed there only a few days. Planes were dropping leaflets ordering everyone to return home, so Paula walked back to Kovno, a trip which took many days and nights. Large numbers of people died along the way.

Upon arrival, all had to register and were afraid to go out of their homes. She met Abe again and also found her youngest brother; one of his hands had been cut off in a factory accident. Deeply depressed, he had one possession which held meaning for him: a pair of handsome boots. One day he was confronted by a group of German soldiers who noticed the boots, shot him, cut off the boots and threw him in a garbage can. He was 18 years old.

In August 1941, Paula was transported to the Kovno Slobotka Ghetto. The half of the Jews who had not been murdered were forced into the ghetto. Those who were able went out to work daily at the air base, always accompanied by German soldiers. One night Paula and Abe were not returned to the ghetto but were shoved into a boxcar, 100 to a car, with only enough room to stand. The presence of a rabbi in the car made them decide to get married. Their destination was the Riga Ghetto. In Latvia, the Germans and Latvians had killed all the Jews except those who had trades and could work. After Riga came Dundega, and then the long march to Kaiserwald, which lasted many days. Those too weak to walk were thrown into the river. At this camp, prisoners dug trenches near the Front, buried the dead and pulled out gold teeth with pliers. Paula's husband Abe had been killed in Latvia.

One night in 1945 Paula had a dream in which her parents spoke to her. The following morning the Russians liberated the camp. In 1946 she traveled to Berlin and then to Fernwald, a Displaced Persons camp in Germany. Here she met Aaron Murawnik and they were married. With the help of UNRRA (United Nations Refugee Resettlement Agency), in 1950, they re-settled in Sioux City, Iowa, where Paula worked in an overall factory until daughter Esther was born. In 1981 they moved to Des Moines. Her husband Aaron worked at several business ventures until retirement.

Born in Gorzda, Lithuania

FRANCES (FRYMETA CHOJKA) SHNURMAN

Frances was born to parents Hinda and Zisldnd Chojka. Frances was the youngest of six children: three girls and three boys. Her father and mother worked in a family-owned bottling company. Frances also worked there until the Germans came in September 1939. The Germans cleared a slum area and converted it into a ghetto. The entire Chojka family was forced into the ghetto along with hundreds of other Jews. In the ghetto there was little food, and what was supplied by the Germans was a thin gruel with almost no nutritional value. It was in the Lodz Ghetto that Frances' parents died of starvation in 1942.

From the ghetto, Frances and her brothers and sisters were shipped out to Auschwitz-Birkenau in cattle cars where they remained for a few days. From there they stopped at several smaller camps, ending up at Stutthof. It was here the siblings were separated. Although Frances tried to locate her siblings after the war, she was unable to find any surviving brothers and sisters. She presumes they were murdered at Stutthof.

Frances remained at Stutthof until close to the war's end. At that time she, along with other survivors, were loaded onto barges and placed in the Baltic Sea with the intent of shipping them to the German port city of Neustadt in Holstein. The barges were bombed however and Frances was one of the few prisoners who survived. She eventually arrived at the intended destination and remained there until liberated by the British Army on May 3, 1945.

A short time later, while going from town to town looking for possible family survivors, Frances arrived at Bergen-Belsen, where she met Meyer Shnurman. Together, still looking for their families, they returned to Neustadt in Holstein, which was a Displaced Persons camp. There they were married in

1945. It was there also that two sons were born in 1946 and 1948. They remained in Neustadt until they emigrated to America in November 1949. The Shnurmans re-settled in Des Moines, where a third son was born in 1953.

Frances worked at Drake University for about eleven years in Food Services until she retired in 1977. She has been in ill health since her days in the camps.

Born in Lodz, Poland

MEYER SHNURMAN

Meyer was born to parents Benjamin and Yetta Shnurman. Meyer had a twin sister as well as one younger sister. His parents worked in a large family-owned textile factory. He attended a technical school, learning the trade of cabinetmaking, as well as attending *cheder* (Jewish religious school).

In September 1939, the Germans invaded Poland, converted a slum area to a ghetto and herded in the Jews. Food was scarce, conditions were crowded and many people died of starvation, including Meyer's parents in 1942. His father was 47 and his mother 45. Crowded boxcars and cattle cars regularly came into Lodz carrying Jews to the ghetto. To reduce the crowded conditions even minimally, large numbers were continually shipped out to Auschwitz as well as to other smaller concentration camps. Also in 1943, Meyer's twin, a nurse, volunteered to help the ill. Instead she was transported out of the ghetto to work on the Autobahn. Meyer later had word that, along with 20 other young women, his sister was thrown into cement mixers and killed. In 1944 he was part of a large group of Jews transported out of the ghetto to Auschwitz-Birkenau, where he remained until about October. His job was to do clean-up work from the burnings in the four crematoria. The memory of this still haunts him.

After this, he was transported to different camps, finally ending up at Braunschweig. The Germans tried to figure out a way to get rid of the prisoners so they wouldn't get caught with the evidence of their crimes. Therefore, since most of the prisoners were barely alive, mere skeletons, they were easily crowded into boxcars where they remained without food or water while being transported to Ludwigslust bei Weberle, outside of Berlin. When they could go no further, they were surrounded by four armies. The following morning, May 2, 1945, they were liberated by the Americans. Ronald (Ubi) Rabinovitz of Des Moines was among Meyer's liberators. The German soldiers had run away.

After the liberation, Meyer went from city to city looking for family members. In his search he went to Bergen-Belsen and there learned his younger sister had been deported from Auschwitz to Stutthof in 1944 and murdered. While in Belsen, he met his future wife, Frances, whom he had known previously. Together they went to Neustadt in Holstein, Germany, where they hoped to find news of Frances' family. No one was found. It was in Neustadt, a Displaced Persons camp, that Meyer and Frances were married in 1945. Sons Benjamin and Jacob were born in 1946 and 1948, respectively.

With the help of UNRRA (United Nations Refugee Resettlement Agency) the family emigrated to America in November 1949. They were re-settled in Des Moines. A third son, Harry, was born in 1953. Meyer worked for Younkers about 21 years until retirement in 1987.

Born in Lodz, Poland

ROSE WALDMAN SZNELER

Rose was the eldest of four children born to Esther and Mordechai (Motel) Waldman: two girls and twin boys. One of the twins died at three months. Rose attended a Polish school. She lived a relatively uncomplicated Jewish life until September 1, 1939, when the Germans invaded Poland and imprisoned the Jews. Although allowed to remain in the city, they were marched to a distribution center where people would call if they needed workers. Rose was sent to work in a clothing factory where she made garments for the German military. Every Friday night prisoners were required to clean the sidewalks. During the week they cleaned the streets.

In 1941 the German police took 500 Jews, including Rose and her family, to a ghetto in Srodula near Sosnowiec, Poland. Every day at 2 a.m. Rose would have to leave for work to get there on time. Soup, their only food, was provided by the Jewish Federation. Then one night, in March 1942, the young women, instead of being taken to their regular jobs, were shoved into cattle cars and transported to Gogolin, a concentration camp. Here factory owners bought prisoners to produce goods for the Germans. Rose remained here for one year.

In 1943 she was shipped out to Gleiwitz-Steigem where they made products used in the manufacture of tires. Her skin was always raw from the soot and intense heat. It was here she learned from a young gentile boy who traveled to Sosnowiec that he had seen 1,000 Jews loaded into boxcars at Srodula and sent to Auschwitz where they were gassed. She assumes her family was gassed. Rose remained in Gleiwitz one year.

The next camp was Blechhammer. She sewed uniforms for the SS for about one year, until in 1945, with news of the

Russians advancing, the Germans ordered them out of the camp. Rose recalls going on a two-week march in freezing January weather. When possible, prisoners slept in barns close to cows for warmth. Every morning people were found frozen to death.

They next were marched to Gross-Rosen, where they remained two weeks, lying about on the floors just waiting to die. It was January and people were naked. Perhaps as many as 100,000 were moved from Gross-Rosen, shipped in boxcars to Buchenwald, Germany, where the men were unloaded. Women were shipped on to Bergen-Belsen because there was no room at Buchenwald.

April 15, 1945, Rose was liberated by the British at Bergen-Belsen. On Rosh Hashanah 1945, Rose Waldman met Jacob Szneler who had come to Belsen searching for his wife and ten-year-old son; both were dead. On March 5, 1946, Jacob and Rose were married in Belsen. It was a Jewish wedding. They remained in Germany and daughter Esther was born in Bremen, April 1947.

With the help of JOINT (Jewish Joint Distribution Committee) and UNRRA (United Nations Refugee Resettlement Agency) they emigrated to the United States in 1950 and were re-settled in Des Moines. Daughter Lola was born in 1952 and son Marvin in 1956. Rose worked for the Iowa Jewish Home and Kneeters. Jacob worked for Midwest Bag until retirement in 1973. Jacob Szneler died January 8, 1994.

Born on. May 11, 1921, in Sosnowiec, Poland

JACOB WAIZMAN

Jacob was born to parents Shloime and Hadasa Waizman in a relatively small town near Krakow. Jacob was the youngest boy in a family of four, and had two brothers and one sister. His father was a Hebrew School teacher, and he now realizes that his mother, a moneylender, was the business-person of the family. As a young man he worked in an uncle's bakery. His brothers worked as painters. Jacob remembers awareness of anti-Semitism, especially between the years 1936 to 1939.

In September 1939, when the Germans invaded Poland, Jacob recalls some Jewish resistance, but within two weeks it was supressed. Jews were then rounded up and forced into a ghetto. His sister escaped to Polish friends and was hidden by them until they were warned that hiding Jews would bring about a sentence of death. They turned her in, and it is assumed she was gassed in Auschwitz. Jacob and his parents remained in the ghetto about one month. His brothers were in the Polish army. One brother died in a mass killing in a nearby forest. The other, a cavalry soldier, was killed after two weeks of fighting.

After the ghetto, Jacob and his parents were transported in boxcars to Auschwitz where they went through the left-right separation: the aged, the non-able-bodied and the children were sent to be gassed while the others went to the right. Jacob never saw his parents again. He remembers Josef Mengele's presence at Auschwitz and the fact that Mangele hit him over the head with a revolver. After three days Jacob was moved out of Auschwitz to Auenrode, Germany.

At this camp the prisoners were forced to work on the Reichsautobahn (RAB) virtually as slave laborers. Jacob remained here for two years. He recalls the cruel treatment there by a kapo, a former family friend. Next he was evacuated to a camp at Johannesdorf, where he also worked on the RAB. Next came Hirschberg for a period of one year where he worked in a wool factory. Acid used in processing the wool affected his eyes.

The 3,000 prisoners who were evacuated from Hirschberg went on a death march for about 21 days to Buchenwald. Hundreds killed themselves or were shot and thrown into the river. Of the 3,000 people who started out, 50 remained, and all but Jacob and a friend went to the gas chamber. They escaped at the last minute by crawling away below the search lights. They hid themselves by lying on a pile of dead bodies until liberated by Patton's 3rd Army on April 11, 1945. Jacob was hospitalized near Weimar for four months, comatose.

Afterwards he went home to Poland where he met Paula Oliwa. They were married April 15, 1946, in Felderfink, Germany. A daughter, Rosa, was born on October 16, 1948, in Wartenberg. They then left for Munich where they remained until HIAS (Hebrew Immigrant Aid Society) assisted them in their resettlement to the United States and Des Moines, Iowa, in May 1950.

Jacob Waizman worked as an assistant engineer for the Des Moines Public Schools until retirement. He is frequently called upon to speak and to remind people that we must never forget.

Born in Zawiercie, Poland

PAULA OLIWA WAIZMAN

Paula was born to parents Rochele and Wolf Oliwa. She was the eldest of four girls. Her father was a tailor and her mother a homemaker. Paula graduated from a Polish school and helped her father as a seamstress.

The Germans invaded Poland in September 1939, but somehow her family was able to remain at home until the end of 1940. Paula was taken first to a camp in Langenbielau, Poland, then to a camp in Klaettendorf, Germany. In the latter camp she managed to bring food in for the inmates while she worked outside. Both of these were forced labor camps.

Around the same time, Paula's parents were deported to Auschwitz along with her two younger sisters. It is assumed that all perished in the gas chambers. One sister survived a concentration camp, the name of which Paula cannot recall. This sister was found in Israel after the war.

Paula was liberated from Klaettendorf, Germany (now Poland), by the Russians in April 1945. She decided to return to Poland for a brief period to seek out family members who might have survived. It was dangerous to return to eastern bloc countries. While there, she met Jacob Waizman through his cousin, and they were married April 15, 1946, in Felderfink, Germany. Their daughter Rosa was born on October 16, 1948. Afterwards they left for Munich where they remained until May 1950 when HIAS (Hebrew Immigrant Aid Society) assisted in their resettlement to Des Moines.

Paula worked for Emco Industries, from which she retired after 30 years of working in production.

Born in Olkusk, Poland

SALLY SZOTLAND WOLF

S ally Sala was born in a small *shtetl* (Jewish village) near Lodz to parents Chaya and Itzhak. They lived in a large apartment complex. Sally was the second youngest of five children: with three brothers and one sister. Her father sold grain and her mother, whom she remembers as a sickly person, was a homemaker. Sally attended a Polish school as well as a Jewish school which she called "Bet Yakov". After completing school, she worked in the home due to her mother's poor health. In late 1938, when rumors were circulating that Hitler was coming to their shtetl, they ran to their grandparents, who had a large house. Their apartment was bombed. It was not too long before Sally's family began wandering to different towns looking for a safe haven where Germans could not find them.

Ultimately, in 1943, Sally and her sister were taken to the Lodz Ghetto. Her mother had died earlier. Sally's brothers were transported elsewhere and never heard from again. While in the ghetto they went to work daily in a factory. Sally worked as a tailor sewing uniforms for the Germans. Her sister died of typhus in the ghetto. In 1944, the prisoners were transported to Auschwitz in boxcars. It took days to get there, with everyone forced to stand because of the crowded conditions. Occasionally people they passed would take pity and throw scraps of bread, otherwise they had no food or water. After arrival at Auschwitz they stayed only one day, after which they were transported to Bergen-Belsen, Germany. Some miles before they got there, they were pushed out of the cars and forced to walk to Belsen. A cousin of Sally's kept forcing her to keep going when she thought she couldn't go any farther.

After three months at Belsen they were sent to Salzwedel, a forced labor camp where they could sleep in barracks. Here they made ammunition until April 14, 1945, when they were liberated by the Americans. Sally recalls only one American entering through the gate. The German officer in command had been so good to them that the prisoners signed a petition to save him. Other officers had wanted to burn the barracks with the prisoners inside so the evidence could be destroyed. The commander had refused to allow this.

Shortly after liberation Sally went to a Displaced Persons camp at Goslar in the Hartz Mountains. It was here that Sally met Mosze Wolfowicz (Morris Wolf), who had learned that his wife and child had been killed. The following year, on June 28, 1946, Sally and Morris were married. Son Ben was born April 17, 1947. In October 1949, with the help of JOINT (Jewish Joint Distribution Committee) and UNRRA (United Nations Refugee Resettlement Agency), the Wolfs were re-settled in Jacksonville, Florida, where they remained for six months. Because of the weather they moved to Des Moines, where their son Harry was born in 1951 and their son Abe in 1955.

Morris Wolf was an expert cabinetmaker and also did business as a builder. Sally helped him in the business. Morris Wolf died February 22, 1995.

Born on March 20, 1925, in Brzeziny, Poland (deceased)

Survivors Who Are Deceased

Mike Baumgarten
1915 - 1978
Auschwitz

Michael Dobrin
1/23/1928 - 2/10/1976
Stutthof

Ansel Fishman
5/6/1920 - 3/14/1970
Dachau

Carolyn Glasman
1926 - 1987
Dachau

Harry Glasman
1915 - 1983
Dachau

Jane Ickowitz
6/27/1929 - 10/13/1989
Moldev

George Jagiello
1913 - 1989
Auschwitz

Fela Mischkiet
4/3/1910 - 3/14/1981
Stutthof

Monek Mischkiet
5/5/06 - 10/31/1980
Dachau

Harry Saltz
Died 1971
Auschwitz

Sol Spiler
5/27/1907 - 6/1/1979
Dachau

Jacob Szneler
1/14/1910 - 1/8/1994
Treblinka-Majdanek

Henry Wolf
1933 - 1990
Auschwitz

Morris Wolf
5/2/1910 - 2/22/1995
Bergen-Belsen

George Zyskind
1929 - 1974
Buchenwald

Illustration by
David Anolik

MEMBERS OF THE DES MOINES AND AMES, IOWA COMMUNITIES WHO ESCAPED HITLER BY FLEEING, WERE IN HIDING, OR WERE SAVED BY RESCUERS.

Esther Bergh, Germany
1939 Kinder transport to England
1941 Israel
1957 Des Moines

Warner Bergh, Germany
1938 Shanghai, China
1957 Des Moines

Ernest Bressler, Austria
1940 Des Moines
1975 Deceased

Stefiy Bressler, Austria
1940 Des Moines (now deceased)

Ann Katzmann, Poland-Austria
1940-1941 Belgium, underground
1950 Des Moines
1983 Deceased

Fred Katzmann, Germany
1939 Fled Germany
1941 Des Moines (now deceased)

Betti Kiess, Germany
1938 Fled Germany
1940 Des Moines (now deceased)

Manuel Kiess, Ukraine
1938 Fled, Germany
1940 Des Moines
1978 Deceased

Simon Krongelb, Poland
Warsaw camp as a Pole
1951 Des Moines
1983 Deceased

Helen Lercher, Poland
Worked for Germans
as Polish maid
1949 Des Moines

Lazar Lercher, Poland
Joined Partisans in woods
1949 Des Moines

Fred Lorber, Austria
1939 Fled to United States
1940 Des Moines
1943-1945 US Army

Ingrid Mazie, Germany
1943 - 1945 East Prussia, hiding
1959 Des Moines

Aaron Murawnik, Poland
Joined Partisans in woods
1981 Des Moines

Simone Soria,
Czechoslovakia - Belgium
1942 Left Brussels; in hiding,
then in Hainaut until
1949, USA
1969 Des Moines (now deceased)

AMES, IOWA

Herbert A. David, Germany
1939 Australia
1972 Ames

Ruth David, Germany
1939 Kindertransport to England
1993 Ames

Vera David, Czechoslovakia
1939 Kindertransport to England
1957 USA
1972 Ames

Hanna Gradwohl, Germany
1937 Brought to
Nebraska, age two
1963 Ames

Jack Horowitz, Austria
1938 Brought to
New York, age seven
1961 Ames

FORMER DES MOINES RESIDENT HOLOCAUST SURVIVORS

Jennie and David
Wolnerman
Auschwitz-Birkenau
Dachau/Bergen-Belsen
1952 USA

OTHER DES MOINES RESIDENT HOLOCAUST SURVIVORS

Phyllis Jagiello
Bergen-Belsen
1949 USA

NOTE ON RESEARCH:

During the 1980s, Adele Anolik of Des Moines directed a project to obtain video testimonials of her husband, Charles, and seven other Des Moines residents who were survivors of the Holocaust. These videotapes were placed at Yale University's Fortunoff Video Archive for Holocaust Testimonials. In 1999, Joanne Rudof, archivist at Yale University's Fortunoff Video Archives, placed a duplicate set of the Des Moines testimonials with the Iowa State Historical Society's Special Collection Unit where they could be more readily viewed by a local audience, especially schools. However, Yale retains copyright. Adele also donated related materials to the Iowa State Historical Society's Special Collections Unit, including her copy of *Mein Kampf* to provide an explanation of how evil in the world can destroy humanity. This collection is available through the Iowa State Historical Society's Library, Tuesday through Friday, 9:30am - 4:30 pm at 600 E. Locust St., Des Moines, Iowa. Those wishing to view the videos are encouraged to call 515-281-6863.

A Note From the Writer:

Although I am not a Holocaust Survivor, I have nevertheless been a part of that community for more than fifty years as the wife of one.

It was my distinct honor and privilege to prepare these histories by interviewing a very special group of people on the occasion of fifty years following the liberation of the concentration camps. Through continued education and knowledge of what occurred, my hope is that nothing like it will occur again.

—Adele Anolik

ADELE WALDNER ANOLIK was born in Kansas City, Kansas, in 1926. She attended Wyandotte High School during years of segregation. After attending the University of Kansas City (now UM-KC) Adele moved to Chicago where she accepted a job as a Registered Medical Technician (#14209) at Mt. Sinai Hospital, eventually becoming Supervisor of the 100-person laboratory. She then met Charles Anolik, a Lithuanian Holocaust survivor, whom she married in 1955. Charles owned Salon Charles in Des Moines, Iowa. Together, they reared three children: Lisa, Julie and David. Lisa, an RN, is married to Dr. David Ikola, a pediatrician in California. Julie, an artist/musician, is married to Martin Cassell, from London, England, a Professor of Anatomy at the University of Iowa, Iowa City, Iowa. David, an artist, is co-owner of Quango, a design corporation in Portland, Oregon and is married to Gabrielle, an artist/librarian. Aside from the challenge of playing chess at Border's weekly, Adele's wishes to be with her four grandchildren: Emily, and Ben in California and Ada and Rueben in Iowa City, Iowa.

The Ice Cube Press began publishing in 1993 to focus on how
to best live with the natural world and to better understand
how people can best live together in the communities they
inhabit. Since then, we've been recognized by a number
of well-known writers, including Gary Snyder, Gene
Logsdon, Michael Pollan, Wes Jackson, Patricia Hampl,
Jim Harrison, Annie Dillard, Kathleen Norris, and Barry
Lopez. We've published a number of well-known authors
as well, including Mary Swander, Jim Heynen, Mary Pipher,
Bill Holm, Carol Bly, Marvin Bell, Debra Marquart, Ted
Kooser, Stephanie Mills, Bill McKibben and Paul Gruchow.
Check out our books at our web site, with booksellers, or
at museum shops, then discover why we are dedicated to
"hearing the other side."

Ice Cube Press
205 N Front Street
North Liberty, Iowa 52317-9302
steve@icecubepress.com
www.icecubepress.com

from high and low, near and far
thanks, hugs, kisses and cheers to
Fenna Marie & Laura Lee
assistants extraordinaire